ISAAC ASIMOV'S NEW LIBRARY OF THE UNIVERSE

A STARGAZER'S GUIDE

BY ISAAC ASIMOV
WITH REVISIONS AND UPDATING BY FRANCIS REDDY

Gareth Stevens Publishing
MILWAUKEE

For a free color catalog describing Gareth Stevens' list of high-quality books, call 1-800-542-2595 (USA) or 1-800-461-9120 (Canada). Gareth Stevens' Fax: (414) 225-0377.

A special thanks to Julian Baum and Richard Baum.

Library of Congress Cataloging-in-Publication Data

Asimov, Isaac.
  A stargazer's guide / by Isaac Asimov; with revisions and updating by
Francis Reddy.
      p. cm. — (Isaac Asimov's New library of the universe)
  Rev. ed. of: The space spotter's guide. 1988.
  Includes bibliographical references and index.
  ISBN 0-8368-1197-6
  1. Astronomy—Observers' manuals—Juvenile literature. 2. Stars—
Observers' manuals—Juvenile literature. [1. Astronomy—Observers'
manuals. 2. Stars—Observers' manuals.] I. Reddy, Francis, 1959-.
II. Asimov, Isaac. The space spotter's guide. III. Title. IV. Series: Asimov,
Isaac. New library of the universe.
QB64.A754 1995
523.8'022'3—dc20   94-34044

This edition first published in 1995 by
Gareth Stevens Publishing
1555 North RiverCenter Drive, Suite 201
Milwaukee, Wisconsin 53212, USA

Project editor: Barbara J. Behm
Design adaptation: Helene Feider
Editorial assistant: Diane Laska
Production director: Susan Ashley
Picture research: Kathy Keller
Artwork commissioning: Kathy Keller and Laurie Shock

Printed in the United States of America

1 2 3 4 5 6 7 8 9 99 98 97 96 95

To bring this classic of young people's information up to date, the editors at Gareth Stevens Publishing have selected two noted science authors, Greg Walz-Chojnacki and Francis Reddy. Walz-Chojnacki and Reddy coauthored the recent book *Celestial Delights: The Best Astronomical Events Through 2001.*

Walz-Chojnacki is also the author of the book *Comet: The Story Behind Halley's Comet* and various articles about the space program. He was an editor of *Odyssey,* an astronomy and space technology magazine for young people, for eleven years.

Reddy is the author of nine books, including *Halley's Comet, Children's Atlas of the Universe, Children's Atlas of Earth Through Time,* and *Children's Atlas of Native Americans,* plus numerous articles. He was an editor of *Astronomy* magazine for several years.

CONTENTS

We live in an enormously large place – the Universe. It's just in the last fifty-five years or so that we've found out how large it probably is. It's only natural that we would want to understand the place in which we live, so scientists have developed instruments – such as radio telescopes, satellites, probes, and many more – that have told us far more about the Universe than could possibly be imagined.

We have seen planets up close. We have learned about quasars and pulsars, black holes, and supernovas. We have gathered amazing data about how the Universe may have come into being and how it may end. Nothing could be more astonishing.

In places away from the bright lights and dust of a big city, we can observe the stars through binoculars and telescopes. In this book, you will discover how to spot some of the wonders of our Solar System, our Galaxy, and beyond!

Isaac Asimov

A Sky of Surprises

If we could stay awake through the night, we would see the stars rise and set. Stars are huge balls of hot gases. The gases light the stars from within. This is unlike planets that shine because of reflected light. The Milky Way, our Galaxy, is home to about two hundred billion stars. And that is just one galaxy. About a hundred billion galaxies exist in the incredibly vast sky.

From night to night, the sky shifts. A pattern of stars seen at midnight on one night won't appear again exactly as it is until an entire year later. The patterns change with the seasons. That's because Earth revolves around the Sun.

Left: In this time-lapse photograph, the Sun, Moon, and stars appear as streaks wheeling across the sky, an illusion caused by the spinning planet on which we live.

5

The Moon's Monthly Travels

As you might guess, the brightest object in the night sky is the Moon. The Moon shines by reflected light from the Sun. The Moon travels around Earth in a little less than a month. In that time, we see its various phases, or shapes.

When the Moon and Sun are on the same side of Earth, we face the Moon's unlighted side. This is the "new Moon," which cannot be seen. The next evening we see a bit of the Moon's sunlit side as a crescent just after sunset. From night to night, the crescent gets thicker until there is a full Moon, and then thinner and thinner until there is a new Moon again.

? *Stonehenge – a prehistoric observatory?*

Before modern astronomical instruments were invented, people had their own ways of watching the stars. In England, there is a circle of large upright stones with other stones in the center. It is called Stonehenge. Some astronomers think Stonehenge might be what is left of a prehistoric observatory. Did ancient astronomers look across the stones to see where the Sun would rise at the summer solstice – or to predict lunar eclipses?

Top: A dramatic shot of our nearest neighbor in space.

Bottom: The phases of the Moon. The Moon's appearance changes as it orbits Earth each month.

New Moon   First Quarter

Gibbous Moon   Full Moon   Gibbous Moon   Last Quarter   Old Moon

The Spring Sky

The next eight pages of this book feature pictures of the sky as seen by an observer looking south. These illustrations feature the stars as seen from the Northern Hemisphere. From the Southern Hemisphere, the stars will appear higher in the sky, and some of the highest stars on the illustrations will not be visible at all.

As you face south, imagine that the top of the picture is folded toward you and passes over your head. The bottom of the picture would then be south, and the top would be north.

As you face south in the spring and look way up over your head, the Big Dipper (part of Ursa Major) will stretch across the sky above you. If you follow the curve of the handle of the Big Dipper back toward the southern part of the sky, you will come upon the constellation Boötes, the Herdsman. One part of Boötes is Arcturus, which is one of the brightest stars in the spring sky.

Continue to follow the imaginary curve south, and you will come to the constellation Virgo, the Maiden, and its bright star, Spica. To the west (right, as you face south) of Virgo is the constellation Leo, the Lion, with its bright star, Regulus.

Virgo and Leo are two of the twelve constellations, or patterns of stars, of what is known as the zodiac. The Sun, Moon, and planets travel through the zodiac as they move across the sky.

Opposite: With the Big Dipper overhead, look for Boötes and the bright star Arcturus in the east, Virgo in the south, and Leo in the west.

Top: The Zodiac of Dendera – a star map of ancient Egypt.

Bottom: Spring in the Northern Hemisphere is Autumn in the Southern Hemisphere.

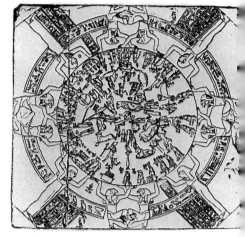

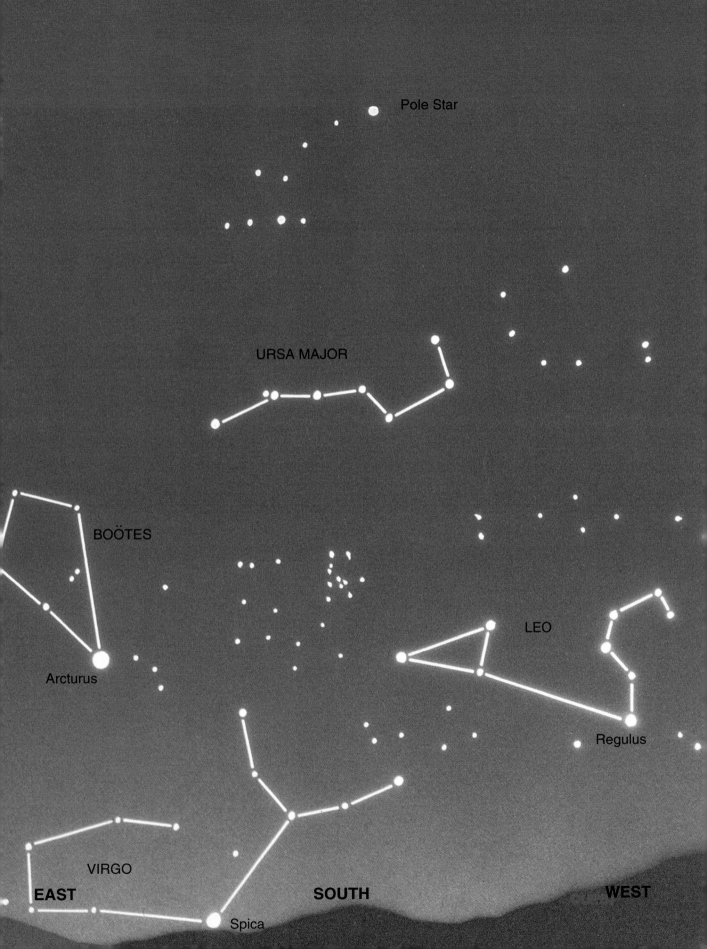

Pole Star

URSA MAJOR

BOÖTES

Arcturus

LEO

Regulus

VIRGO

EAST

SOUTH

WEST

Spica

The Summer Sky

One of the easiest constellations to spot in the summer sky is Sagittarius, the Archer. Its outline looks like a teapot in the southern sky.

The Milky Way is visible as a band of foggy light encircling the sky. It passes through Sagittarius and is brightest there. With the use of even a small telescope, you can see many stars in the Milky Way.

To the west, to the right of Sagittarius as you face south, is a curve of stars. This constellation is Scorpius, the Scorpion, with its bright red star Antares. Antares is a red giant, hundreds of times wider than our Sun.

Over your head as you face south, and halfway between Sagittarius and Polaris (the North Star), is Lyra, the Lyre, with its bright star, Vega. To the east of Lyra is Cygnus, the Swan, with its bright star, Deneb. Halfway between Deneb and Sagittarius is the bright star Altair, in Aquila, the Eagle. The three stars Vega, Deneb, and Altair form a star pattern known as the Summer Triangle.

Opposite: Lyra shines overhead, with Cygnus off to the east and Aquila to the south. Farther south and west lie Sagittarius and Scorpius.

Top: Sagittarius, the Archer.

Bottom: Summer in the Northern Hemisphere is Winter in the Southern Hemisphere.

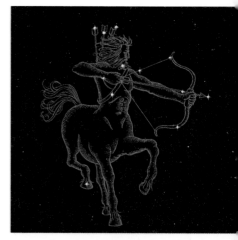

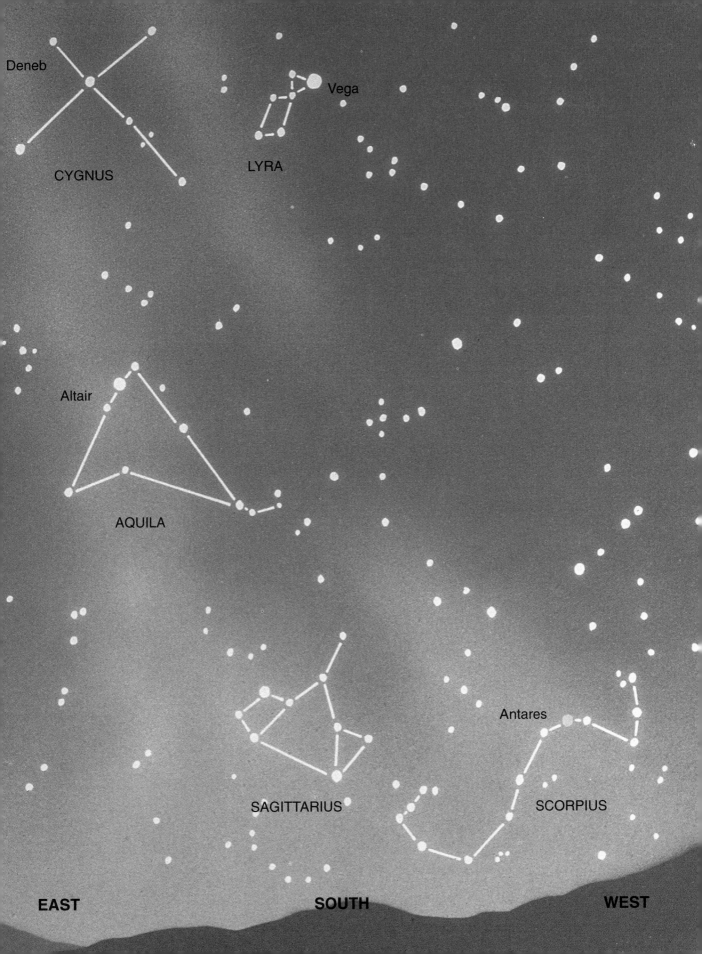

The Autumn Sky

The constellation Pegasus, the Flying Horse, is high in the autumn sky (nearly overhead as you face south). Its four bright stars form the Square of Pegasus. Immediately to its northeast (above and to the left of Pegasus), is Andromeda, the Chained Maiden. Within Andromeda, you can spot a small, foggy patch of light. When observed through a telescope, this patch turns out to be a huge collection of stars called the Andromeda Galaxy.

To the southeast of Pegasus (lower left as you face south) is Cetus, the Whale, which has a rather dim star that is variable. A variable star grows brighter, then dimmer. When astronomers first saw this star, the changing brightness seemed so unique that they named the star *Mira*, which means "wonderful."

Opposite: Three large constellations dominate the autumn sky – Pegasus, Andromeda, and Cetus.

Top: Andromeda contains the farthest object visible to the unaided eye – galaxy M31, the Andromeda Galaxy. Its light travels over two million years before reaching Earth.

Bottom: Autumn in the Northern Hemisphere is Spring in the Southern Hemisphere.

❓ How far in the sky can we see?

The most distant object we can see clearly without a telescope is the Andromeda Galaxy. It looks like a dim, fuzzy star, but it is actually a galaxy larger than our own Milky Way. It is over two million light-years away. We can see even farther with a telescope. For instance, the nearest quasar is about a billion light-years away, and other quasars might be 17 billion light-years away. Astronomers do not expect to see many things much farther away than that!

ANDROMEDA
Galaxy M31

PEGASUS

CETUS

Mira

EAST   **SOUTH**   **WEST**

The Winter Sky

In the winter sky, you can see Orion, the Hunter. This beautiful constellation can help identify other star groups in the winter sky, as well. On Orion's northeastern edge (the upper left, as you face south) is the huge red giant star called Betelgeuse. Orion's southwestern edge (lower right) is marked by Rigel, a star about 55,000 times brighter than our Sun.

Between these two bright stars is a row of three stars called Orion's belt. Below the belt is another row of stars, Orion's sword. The middle "star" of the sword is actually a huge cloud of gas and dust called the Orion Nebula. Orion's belt points down and to the left (southeast) at the bright star Sirius, in Canis Major, the Great Dog. Sirius is the brightest star visible from Earth – not counting our Sun, of course!

The belt also points up and to the right (north-west) toward Aldebaran, the brightest star in Taurus, the Bull.

Opposite: Sirius, the brightest star in the sky besides our Sun, gleams in the southeast. Rigel and Aldebaran, nearly due south, shine higher up.

Top: The Orion Nebula is a giant gas cloud in which stars are born.

Bottom: Winter in the Northern Hemisphere is Summer in the Southern Hemisphere.

? *Did Sirius change color?*

Certain ancient writers described Sirius as being red in color. In reality, Sirius is a brilliant white star. Could it have been red in ancient times and later turned white? Astronomers don't see how. The ancient Egyptians watched Sirius rise with the Sun so they would know when the Nile River was going to flood. When Sirius rose, it may have looked reddish, just as the Sun does. That may have been why ancient people thought of Sirius as being red.

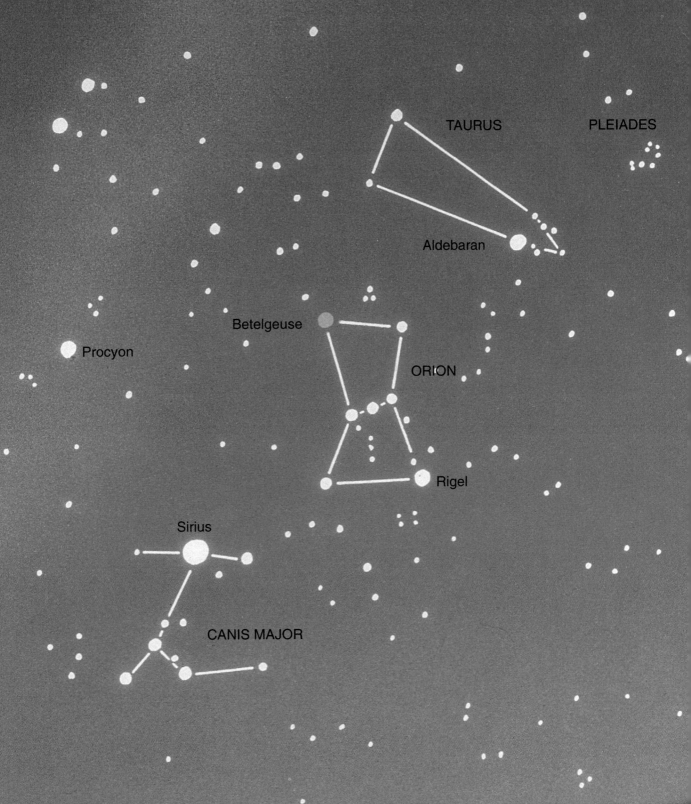

TAURUS   PLEIADES

Aldebaran

Betelgeuse

ORION

Procyon

Rigel

Sirius

CANIS MAJOR

EAST   **SOUTH**   **WEST**

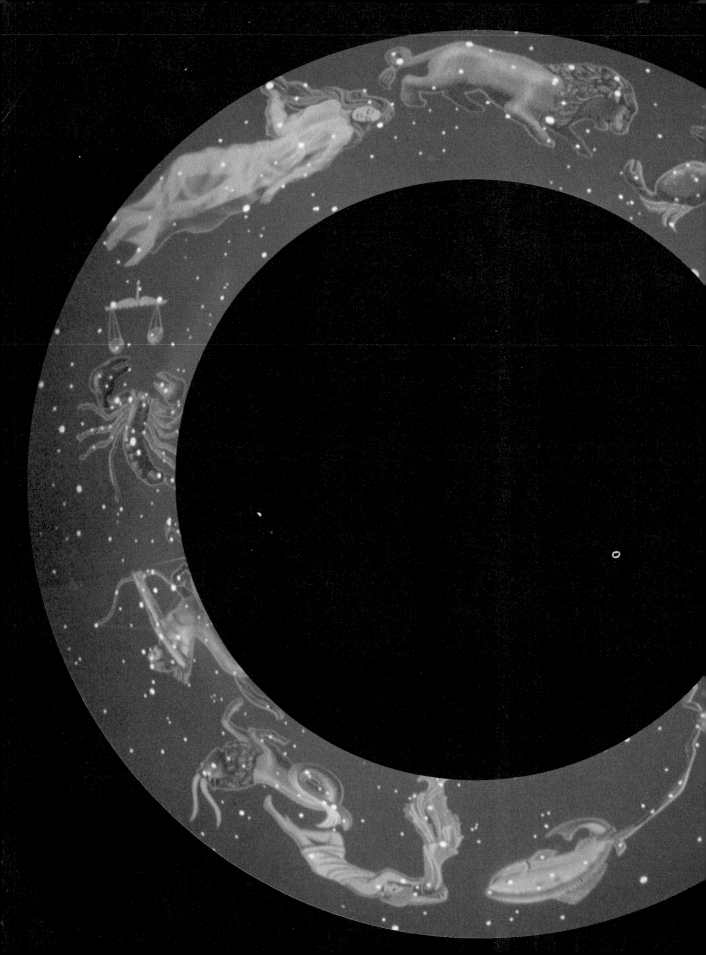

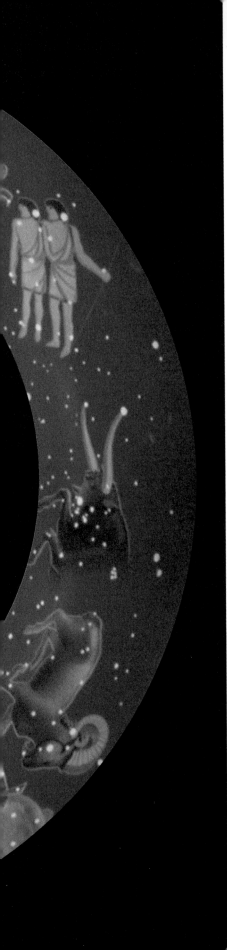

Heavenly Journeys

Not all the objects in the sky turn in one group or follow the same path.

The Moon moves across the sky through the twelve constellations of the zodiac, making a complete circle in a little less than a month. The Sun moves along the same path. But it moves much more slowly, staying in each constellation of the zodiac for one month and making a complete circle in a year.

Five bright, starlike objects – Mercury, Venus, Mars, Jupiter, and Saturn – also move along the zodiac. These planets take different lengths of time to move across the sky. For example, Jupiter takes about twelve years to circle the sky, while Saturn takes more than twenty-nine.

Left: The zodiac constellations, *(clockwise from the top)* are Leo (the lion), Cancer, Gemini, Taurus, Aries, Pisces, Aquarius, Capricorn, Sagittarius, Scorpius, Libra, and Virgo.

Below: As Earth moves in its yearly orbit around the Sun, it is the Sun that appears to move against the background of stars in the sky. The constellations it moves through make up the zodiac.

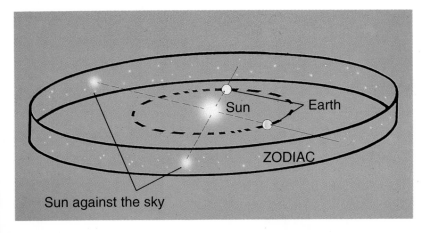

Sun against the sky

The Sun's Nearest Neighbors

Venus and Mercury are closer to the Sun than Earth. For that reason, we always notice them near the Sun. We cannot see them in the daytime. They only become visible to us shortly after sunset or shortly before sunrise.

When Venus appears in the western sky, it's often the first "star" we notice as evening falls. At these times, Venus is called the Evening Star. When it is on the other side of the Sun, Venus shines in the eastern sky in the hours before dawn as the Morning Star. Venus is the third brightest object in the sky, after the Sun and Moon. Mercury is much harder to see than Venus. Because Mercury never moves far from the Sun, we cannot see it in a dark sky.

Opposite: A naked-eye view of Mercury, Venus, and a crescent Moon. Mercury and Venus go through a cycle of phases each month, just like the Moon.

Below: Venus is covered by a thick atmosphere that hides its surface from human eyes, but not from the human mind. This photo of Venus was taken by the *Magellan* spacecraft. The planet's face is revealed using a new type of radar.

The Farthest Planets

Mars, Jupiter, and Saturn are all farther from the Sun than Earth is. They all shine in the midnight sky. Since we only see their sunlit portions, they always appear "full" when observed from Earth.

Jupiter and Saturn are giant planets. Through a telescope, Jupiter is seen as a small globe, along with its four natural satellites, or moons. Saturn has many bright rings. The rings are formed by countless pieces of rock and ice that circle the planet. These magnificent rings make Saturn one of the sky's most beautiful sights.

There are still farther planets – Uranus, Neptune, and Pluto. You can see Uranus and Neptune easily with a small telescope, but you need a more powerful one to see Pluto.

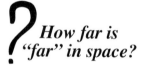 *How far is "far" in space?*

The farthest known planet in the Solar System is Pluto. Traveling at 186,000 miles (300,000 kilometers) a second, light takes about 5 1/2 hours to reach Earth from Pluto. The nearest star (after our Sun), Alpha Centauri, is so far away that its light takes 4.3 years to reach us. We say it is 4.3 light-years away. Our Milky Way Galaxy, a huge collection of stars shaped like a pinwheel, is about 100,000 light-years from end to end!

Top: Saturn, the ringed beauty.

Center: Jupiter, the largest known planet.

Bottom: Mars, "the red planet."

Opposite: Jupiter *(upper right)* and Venus, together with a young Moon.

Two Types of Telescopes

At first, a good pair of binoculars will be fine for viewing the heavens. You will be able to see great views of the Milky Way and stars ten times too faint for your eyes alone. But you can do all this and more with a telescope!

Telescopes collect light from an object in space, bring the light into focus, and magnify the image that is produced. There are two types of telescopes – refracting and reflecting. Refractors use lenses, and reflectors use mirrors. Most of the time, refracting telescopes are used to study the planets and the Moon, and reflecting telescopes are used to study objects outside our Galaxy.

Whichever type of telescope you choose will allow you to be astonished by the sights overhead. You will be able to observe artificial satellites, study the surface of the Moon, and see comets in glorious detail.

Below and opposite top:
A refracting telescope contains a large lens that collects and focuses light to the eyepiece.

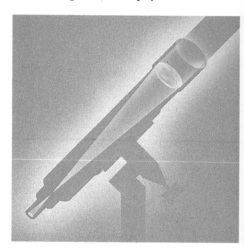

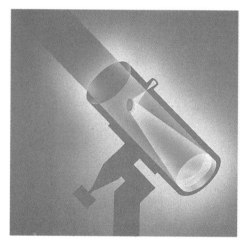

Above and opposite bottom:
A reflecting telescope contains a large mirror that bounces and focuses light onto a smaller mirror, which bounces the light to the eyepiece.

! *The tiniest stars pack a powerful punch!*

Some stars are pushed together so tightly that they are smaller than our Earth, but contain as much matter as our Sun. One such type of star is white-hot, and it is called a white dwarf. But even tighter, smaller stars exist. For instance, if all the particles in our Sun, which is 860,000 miles (1.39 million km) in diameter were pushed together until they touched, the Sun would be only 8 miles (13 km) across. Stars like this are called neutron stars.

Our Vast Universe

The stars we see with our eyes alone are only the nearest stars. With telescopes, we can see objects much farther away.

You can see star clusters, each of which may contain thousands of stars. The largest star cluster is in the constellation Hercules.

You can also use a telescope to see distant galaxies that lie far beyond our Milky Way. The Andromeda Galaxy is one of the closest galaxies. Some galaxies look like oval pieces of fog and are called elliptical galaxies. Some look like pinwheels and are called spiral galaxies.

Even a small telescope will give you an idea of the vastness of the Universe!

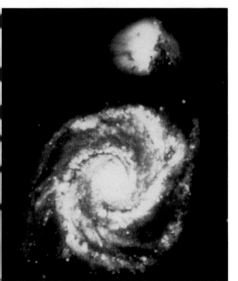

Opposite: The Helix Nebula is a faint shell of gas blown from an aging star.

Left: From Earth, the spiral Whirlpool Galaxy (M51) looks like a fuzzy pinwheel.

Below: Our neighbor, the Andromeda Galaxy.

! *Even astronomers can't always believe their eyes!*

About a hundred years ago, an astronomer saw a small moon of Saturn that was never seen again. Perhaps it was an error or maybe there was a flaw in the telescope. In 1937, an asteroid was spotted flying just 500,000 miles (800,000 km) from Earth. It has never been seen again. Sometimes, astronomers see small changes on the Moon, which is supposedly a dead world. Are these mistakes, or is the Moon not quite dead? The sky is full of mysteries – even today!

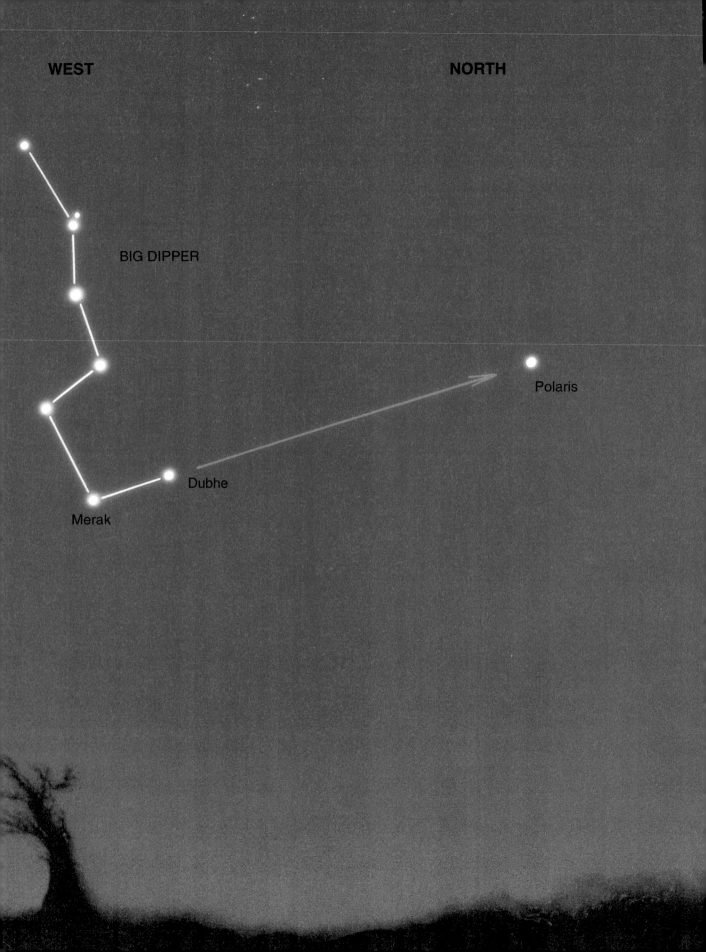

WEST

NORTH

BIG DIPPER

Polaris

Dubhe

Merak

EAST

CASSIOPEIA

Fact File: Constellations of the Northern Hemisphere

In the Northern Hemisphere, stars turn in large circles around a star called Polaris. Polaris is also called the North Star because it constantly stays in the North, almost directly above Earth's North Pole.

From the Northern Hemisphere, certain constellations can be seen circling Polaris. They never set and are always visible.

The seven stars of the Big Dipper are in the chief northern constellation Ursa Major, the Great Bear. The two stars at the bowl end of the dipper are called the "pointers." Follow an imaginary line through them to find Polaris. On the other side of Polaris from the Big Dipper are five stars in a *W* shape. This constellation is Cassiopeia, the Queen.

Left: The Big Dipper and Cassiopeia are visible throughout the year in the Northern Hemisphere.

Below: If you look in the northern sky at the same time each night for a year, you will see the Big Dipper and Cassiopeia slowly chase each other around Polaris, the North Star.

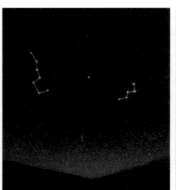

Winter

Spring

Summer

Autumn

27

Fact File: Constellations of the Southern Hemisphere

Many of the constellations of the Northern Hemisphere were mapped a very long time ago. They were named after the gods and heroes of ancient Greek mythology or after objects that were in common use in ancient times.

However, the sky in the Southern Hemisphere was not mapped until much later. It was mapped because explorers needed information about the southern sky in order to navigate their ships at night. So when astronomers gave names to the constellations of the Southern Hemisphere, they did not use names from ancient myths. Instead, they named the constellations after the animals found in explorers' travels and the instruments they used to find their way amid the sea and stars.

When humans travel to distant planets, stars, and galaxies in the future, the star patterns seen from their point of view will be different from the constellations we know from Earth. What will they name their constellations after?

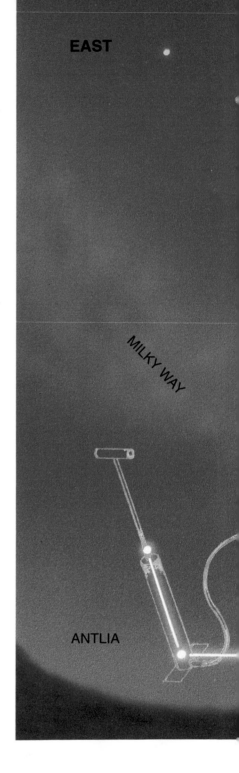

Name of Constellation	Description	Named by	Year
Dorado Tucana Apus	Goldfish Toucan Bird of Paradise	Johann Bayer (Germany)	1603
Circinus Horologium Antlia Telescopium	Compasses Clock Air Pump Telescope	Nicholas Louis Lacaille (France)	1750s

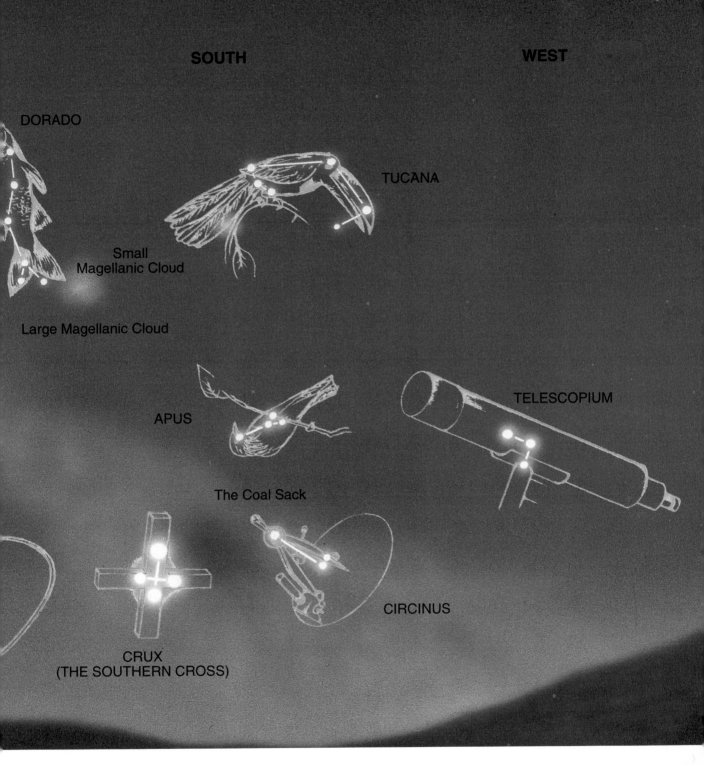

SOUTH

WEST

DORADO

TUCANA

Small
Magellanic Cloud

Large Magellanic Cloud

APUS

TELESCOPIUM

The Coal Sack

CIRCINUS

CRUX
(THE SOUTHERN CROSS)

Above: A view of the sky in the Southern Hemisphere showing some of the constellations featured in the chart *(opposite).* A constellation called the Southern Cross, or Crux, points to the place the southern stars circle around. It is opposite Polaris. The Southern Cross is a key constellation for navigating south of the Equator.

More Books about Astronomy

Astronomy in Ancient Times. Asimov (Gareth Stevens)
Astronomy Basics. Litpak (Prentice-Hall)
Far Out: How to Create Your Own Star World. West (Carolrhoda Books)
Find the Constellations. Rey (Houghton Mifflin)
Galaxies. Simon (Morrow)
Night Sky. Barrett (Franklin Watts)
Night Sky Book. Jobb (Little, Brown)
Peterson First Guide to Astronomy. Pasachoff (Houghton Mifflin)
Sun Dogs and Shooting Stars: A Skywatcher's Calendar. Branley (Houghton Mifflin)

Video

Our Solar System. (Gareth Stevens)

Places to Visit

You can map the planets and stars without leaving Earth. Here are some museums, observatories, and planetariums where you can stargaze.

Hayden Planetarium
Museum of Science
Science Park
Boston, MA 02114-1099

Henry Crown Science Center
Museum of Science and Industry
57th Street and Lake Shore Drive
Chicago, IL 60637

Seneca College Planetarium
1750 Finch Avenue East
North York, Ontario M2J 2X5

Perth Observatory
Walnut Road
Bickley, W.A. 6076 Australia

Places to Write

Here are some places you can write for more information about stargazing. Be sure to state what kind of information you would like. Include your full name and address so they can write back to you.

Jet Propulsion Laboratory
Public Affairs 180-201
4800 Oak Grove Drive
Pasadena, CA 91109

Canadian Space Agency
Communications Department
6767 Route de L'Aeroport
Saint Hubert, Quebec J3Y 8Y9

Sydney Observatory
P. O. Box K346
Haymarket 2000 Australia

National Space Society
922 Pennsylvania Avenue SE
Washington, D.C. 20003

NASA Lewis Research Center
Educational Services Office
21000 Brookpark Road
Cleveland, OH 44135

The Planetary Society
65 North Catalina
Pasadena, CA 91106

Glossary

Andromeda Galaxy: a huge collection of stars in the constellation Andromeda that can be seen with a telescope.

billion: the number represented by 1 followed by nine zeroes – 1,000,000,000. In some countries, this number is called a "thousand million." In these countries, one billion would then be represented by 1 followed by twelve zeroes – 1,000,000,000,000 – a million million.

constellation: a grouping of stars in the sky that seems to trace out a familiar pattern, figure, or symbol.

galaxy: any of the many large groupings of stars, gas, and dust that exist in the Universe. Our Galaxy is known as the Milky Way.

gibbous: the Moon when more than half, but not the entire shape, is lit.

moon: a natural satellite that revolves around a planet.

new Moon: the phase of the Moon where the side not lit by the Sun faces Earth. Since we see none of the sunlight reflected by the Moon, we cannot see the Moon at this time. It's the opposite of a full moon, the phase where the side facing us is fully lit by the Sun.

Northern Hemisphere: the half of Earth north of the Equator.

observatory: a structure designed for watching and recording celestial objects and events.

phases: the periods when Venus, Mercury, and our Moon are partly lit by the Sun. It takes about one month for Earth's Moon to progress from full Moon back to full Moon.

pointers: the two stars at the "bowl" end of the Big Dipper that point toward Polaris, the North Star.

prehistoric: the period in history before writing was used.

pulsar: a neutron star that sends out rapid pulses of light or other radiation.

quasar: the starlike core of a galaxy that may have a large black hole at its center.

red giant: a huge star that develops when the hydrogen in an aging star runs low and the extra heat makes the star expand. The outer layers then change to a cool red.

reflector: a type of telescope that uses mirrors.

refractor: a type of telescope that uses lenses.

revolve: to go around completely, or circle, just as Earth revolves around the Sun.

Southern Hemisphere: the half of Earth south of the Equator.

Stonehenge: a place in southwestern England that may have been an ancient observatory.

Universe: all existing things, including Earth, the Sun, the Solar System, galaxies, and all that which is or may be beyond.

variable star: a star whose light grows brighter, then dimmer, then brighter again.

zodiac: the band of twelve constellations across the sky that represents the paths of the Sun, the Moon, and all the main planets except Pluto.

Index

Born in 1920, Isaac Asimov came to the United States as a young boy from his native Russia. As a young man, he was a student of biochemistry. In time, he became one of the most productive writers the world has ever known. His books cover a spectrum of topics, including science, history, language theory, fantasy, and science fiction. His brilliant imagination gained him the respect and admiration of adults and children alike. Sadly, Isaac Asimov died shortly after the publication of the first edition of *Isaac Asimov's Library of the Universe*.

The publishers wish to thank the following for permission to reproduce copyright material: front cover, © Frank Zullo; 4-5, © Anglo-Australian Telescope Board, David Malin, 1980; 6-7 (upper), © Frank Zullo; 6-7 (lower), Lick Observatory Photographs; 8 (upper), Courtesy of Julian Baum; 8 (lower), New York State Department of Economic Development; 9, © Julian Baum 1988; 10 (upper), Science Photo Library; 10 (lower), New York State Department of Economic Development; 11, © Julian Baum 1988; 12 (upper), National Optical Astronomy Observatories; 12 (lower), New York State Department of Economic Development; 13, © Julian Baum 1988; 14 (upper), NASA; 14 (lower), New York State Department of Economic Development; 15, © Julian Baum 1988; 16-17, © Brad Greenwood, Courtesy of Hansen Planetarium; 17, © Matthew Groshek; 18, © Frank Zullo; 19, NASA/JPL; 20 (upper and center), NASA; 20 (lower), © California Institute of Technology, 1965; 21, © Frank Zullo; 22 (both), © Matthew Groshek; 23 (both), Meade Instruments; 24-25, © Anglo-Australian Telescope Board, David Malin, 1979; 25 (upper), NASA; 25 (lower), © California Institute of Technology, 1959; 26-27, 27 (all), © Julian Baum 1988; 28-29, © Julian Baum and Matthew Groshek, 1988.

Elmwood School
3025 Ezra Ave.
Zion, Illinois 60099